Outside the Institution

LARS AMUND VAAGE

Outside the Institution
— *Selected Poems* —

Shearsman Books
Exeter

First published in the United Kingdom in 2010 by
Shearsman Books Ltd
58 Velwell Road
Exeter EX4 4LD

www.shearsman.com

ISBN 978-1-84861-075-0

Acknowledgements
The author and publisher would like to thank Forlaget Oktober, Oslo,
for permission to publish these translations.
The poems first appeared in the following collections:
Det andre rommet (2001) and *Utanfor institusjonen* (2006).
Thanks also to Longhouse Publishers of Vermont for publishing earlier
versions of some of the translations in the two folder booklets,
The Sheep Farmer Poems (2007) and *The Institution Poems* (2008)

This translation has been published
with the financial support of NORLA.

CONTENTS

From *The Other Room*

From *Outside the Institution*

Outside the Institution

from *The Other Room*

Behind the word there is shadow

Behind the word there is shadow
Behind the shadow a farm with house and trees
Behind the trees a bright, green field
thought cannot reach

Look, you who come walking

Look, you who come walking
You who are alive, you
who have strayed
all the way out here
See the houses, the painting
so many layers
You who come so near
See old boards, the borders of houses
and rotten handles
on something that once had
a name. Something mineral
An opening
A door that swings
on the outskirts of the heart

You who live and can love

You who live and can love
long, untamed and forget
who you are
See the meat hanging
on the wall, drier than twigs

Look further, behind the house
in a room out there
in the open, it collapsed
when you put your foot down

Behind your eyes
Behind a distance
dear one
Far away over there
Make a leap
Behind water, reeds
behind the rooms in the hay
women rest
Sleep has chased them
to Andromeda

Behind loss there is another loss

Behind loss there is another loss
but less distinct
Under the farmyard is an other farmyard
not yet excavated
No one knows
where the old house stood
No one hears the dogs
bite off slivers of bone
with their canines
You shall find
invisible post holes
under the grass

You do not need to build

You do not need to build
anything for me
I built these rooms myself
from nails and snow
I would rather you shut out the day
Took rooms away

BEHIND THE TREES

Behind the trees, shadows
waver slowly
from sun and time
Behind the fence that has fallen down
lush ferns, sweet peas
Behind branches, what was
covered
needles, leaves
and further down to a dark room
of air
Behind the wind, hills, the horizon
hollows left by humans
near crags, cliffs
There was I
Behind the curtain that fell
so unexpectedly
The applause had silenced
The wind stilled
I was on the endless
back stage, painted black
so the walls did not show
Distances did not exist anymore
I was there
not in thought
nor body
but with the sense of smell, oblivion
skin
Detected
the burnt stench of
searchlights
The lamp filaments went cold
I walked along the wall

groping my way
reading structures
synthetic fibre, plaster
and old wood
Suddenly I was inside the wall
I did not cough from the mineral wool
or dust
Nothing itched
or pinched me
I swam as in a fluid
I kicked my feet slowly
swallowing and swallowing
something soft

My mother cried

My mother cried
in the distance between me and another woman
My mother cried in the empty space
not to be understood, not to be reached
My mother cried hot
and dry
My mother cried, I thought, I believed, because
a woman was with me
who could not see
me

O, mother in mist, mother in oatmeal
mornings long ago
You placed everything away
in mountainsides

Mother in twigs, in tassels
Mother in the sweepings from the winter
fire wood on a floor. You
knew less than dust and trash
thrown around by children
but you cried

You drew black tree tops against the sky
with the India ink pens
I got for Christmas
once
You said the light blue
was not for me

A woman was near me

A woman was near me
lived with me
walked with me
very near my arm
without stumbling

I left her
She left me
(often)
Still she accompanied me
loyal, beautiful, dumb
with patience

She said nothing, came to me
stayed with me
leant against me, through
the days, years
like a whale calf
almost like mother

Like mother, mother
she said without laughing
I did not understand
I was young
And laughed back at her

Her children were in me
before they were in her

A woman left me

A woman left me
every day
She walked faster than me
She was fitter. She was more silent
She did not spend too much time
on questions

When I was by the garage, and the mailbox
where the dead bird lay
she was already in the house

She used whatever she found
to keep quiet
even doors, messages of wood
that opened one last time
for her hands

She sprang up the stairs inside
she climbed the spine
lit by electric suns
She threw off her shawls and tentacles
to one who might come by
some other time

She escaped to the roof
tottering along the ridge
Her steps on the tiles died
out
Boughs and cones from the farmyard tree
rushed from the eaves
And it was night

And it was morning
the next day
When I bent down
to light the stove
I heard
her breathing through the chimney

The other room

1 I entered the other room
because it was empty
Not because I left the others
but in order to return

On the door there was a white hand
trace of an extinct bird

2 I entered the other room
every day, every year, always
Was there a door? An opening?
Was there a flicker
of birth and light?

Deep in the room I saw:
The floor was ice
Dust lay on the shelves

The smells were: honey, deep chairs
damp

3 I never entered the other room
alone, because others accompanied me
in spirit
or so I thought

I dragged the others with me
like petals on roses
that I pulled apart

I was the destroyer of life
the one who fled the kitchen

4   There was nothing for me in the other room
    There was nothing for me in the first
    I had no plan, no task
    in the first room
    I stood there empty handed
    until I left

    I wanted them to see me leave
    I returned
    after they had left

5   I did not want them to ask
    what I wanted there
    But I wished them to believe
    I had an errand
    Not only emptiness
    Not just wasted time
    I was time's destroyer

    I was the seer of the other room

6   Far away
    far out by the wall
    of white frost, dissolved

into food and soap
they noticed me
as I rested a moment
by the sill, at the entrance
before I went in

7　When I came out of the other room
the first room was
also empty
The others were out on the road
in the street
where stones lay
along hedges of spiraea
All grass grew the same way
towards them

Walnut stained their fingers brown
Their blood was green
They showed their hands
some like flags
others like wooden spatulas
and said they needed
neither time nor space
while they thought about eternity

8　What could I do
but leave both rooms, the first, the second

my entrance and exit, Lord
Jesus Christ, my God
and follow them
into the light?

They turned and looked as I approached
under the sky
The rooms
no longer existed

THE HAYLOFT

I was in the hayloft
Outside the air was clear, blue
above the yard
The hayloft was the third room
the furthest. Closed
off to the world
A narrow ray of light
blinded me

I walked there slowly
dragging lines
rope, snakes
through the heather
whispering after me

I climbed over beams, red
boards, piping
that burst
but made my way
into the back of summer
empty dovecots
and remnants of egg

The dust had settled
The floor boards slippery with secretion
from stored grass

Below my feet the barn, cold
and empty because it was summer
The cows were out, hardened layers of dung
bore witness

The memory of their heavy bodies and
calm deep breathing
reached me like punishment

THE SHEEP FARMER

I like sheep farmers
sheep farmers like small things
frail animals, not as round
as the thick wool
would suggest

Sheep farmers have small houses
and low barns
With watery grey walls
and silver roofs
they are at one with the ground

Sheep farmers throw food to their flock
in the old wooden basin
They hand out the grain feed
with a measuring cup
Those heavy with lamb
get most

The sheep farmers are done
in the cold shed
Evening has come and they stand
a while by the switch
before they turn off the light
and grope their way out
in the dense darkness

Around the sheepcote there are
imprints of hooves no bigger than
a deer's foot
In the black mud you can also see
the farmer's own footprints
Straighter
than the small ones
and with more intent
the farmer moves
between the house and barn

Ask for the farmer
He is invisible
He is gone just like his animals
They are inside the half-darkened
cold room
Where is the farmer?
His traces are in the snow
His boots
are clean as air

The farmer travels to a show
with five ewes and four lambs
He does not go because
he wants a career
He loves all the animals equally
He doesn´t eat them
just like that
He goes away to a show
to have a taste of the hot broth
they serve
in a sports ground
A thousand strange sheep
await him
in the bitter autumn weather

The farmer looks at the lambs
Their childhood is not
yet over
The farmer too wants to play
His feet
shake and rattle
in his oversized rubber boots

He drives home with the sheep
on his trailer
The prize bows they received
red and yellow
flutter lightly
in the wind

At home it does not seem as if
the sheep recognize the place
They don't want to go into the cote
They tumble and run around in the brown
the grey
They trample in the mud
They run among rocks
The farmer lives alone

Behind the wind
behind the horizon
behind the light that moves away
the farmer stands
He looks around the patch of land
at the edge of the woods
by the wall the ancestors put up
with fingers
like tender claws

He left his home
walked across the yard
small slopes
outer space
Something took hold of him
and contracted in him
like the hearts of farm machinery

Once he moved into empty houses
with grand gestures
and pulled mother and father
out into open air
God's own church
so that they could die there

He saved money, but
when he had enough, no woman wanted
to come and see him buy
all the usual stuff
at the co-op

He was tossed around
inside his own skull
as if his head was the vault of heaven
but he didn't notice

Who was the farmer?
Who was this old man
with the discoloured hands?

Who was it that got him to the hospital?
Who nursed him there?
Who put ointment on his eyelids
so that he should never see again?
Who did not come to visit?
He didn't know
It never crossed his mind
because a nonexistent hand
rubbed it all out

He didn't suffer any loss
He lost nothing
Everything was the same
Everything lying still
in his yard

The sheep farmer didn't capture the wild sheep
didn't tame them, no
didn't ruin anything for them
The sheep farmer moved in with them
one morning long ago
gently he built
a house, a barn
and a fold no wild sheep
could fear

The sheep farmer didn't say much
to the wild sheep
but listened to them
Copied their habits
and gestures
and behaved like them
among children

The sheep farmer worked the soil carefully
He let the field grow as old as
a memory of summer
He honoured the vital plants
dock, couch grass, ground elder
He gathered sweet gale in the rough grazing
for his beer
He drove tractors
light as gliders
across the fields that were
sketched by women
he thought about
The grass did not bend
under his boots
The sheep busy
with thoughts of their own
The sheep ate
more and more of him

Now it is the sheep that are invisible
They run the farm now
They took over
more and more of the operations
They set up annual plans
and hid them somewhere
inside the house
in the bottom of a chest
or outside
behind the yard, the rotary hoe, the plough
the hay tedder, all the old
tools left out to rust

The farmer comes over the hill
He is not driving a tractor anymore
He is driving his thoughts
further on

Once the young sheep farmer followed
the bells
he heard in the mountains
Sweet fern tickled
his naked calves
His thighs stung
as he went uphill

He was wearing blue trousers
that were too small
A jacket with a zip
He didn't sweat like other people
the skin seemed dry

He met only
unfamiliar sheep
They looked at him
with pure faces
He gave them salt, lickstone
and old bread crust he moistened
in his mouth

What did the sheep farmer think?
He who turned around and walked
How could his houses
float above the hill
or sometimes be tangled
in shadows
of coppice, sun and wind?
Why didn't the locals
search for him?
Didn't they know
all the flat boulders
hollow logs
and small clearings in the rough grazing?
Why didn't they take down
his curtains
instead of letting them hang
like cobwebs in the woods?
Why was it always the locals
that crossed his yard
and not the farmer himself?
The inheritance was his, he got everything
from dead souls
Why didn't anyone write songs about him
for feast days like Confirmation?
Why didn't they approach him
long after
as he stood
turning his head by a shelf
in the big store?
They did not know him
They didn't take up his inheritance
What he left them
was wet wood

The wild sheep never forgot the sheep farmer
The wild sheep also learnt something
from him
The wild sheep carried the sheep farmer
over the windswept slopes of naked rock
on the flat islands
The wild sheep ran
along the beaches smelling of
crushed crab
Far away:
coils of rope
fish factories
low mountains resembling plastic
When he died the sheep farmer
released the wild sheep

In spring the sheep farmer sent
his sheep to the mountains
The snow hardly gone from the heights
after hard winters

Only once did the sheep farmer
go with them there
on a stranger's truck

Several herds in the same load
The farmer stood up at the back of the truck
with wind in his hair
the driver's cabin packed
with other farmers

The sheep farmer watched the road disappear
beneath the hood of the car
Rigid trucks
accelerate across the land
he thought

In autumn he brought the sheep home again
Like shepherds on the fields of Bethlehem
only with larger gestures
louder calls
They were deep in the mountains
Summers were calmer
where the sheep farmer lived
than in the Holy Land

He gathered them
He herded them together
and got them home before the autumn dark
All he could find
he rushed into
the safe house

He walked across the mountain
with many other
sheep farmers
If they spotted a white patch far away
maybe more
the sheep farmer could capture them
He ran after the ram
until he overpowered it
The sheep turned over
and pulled his legs
under him
breathing like a bird
The farmer also threw himself down
bent his fingers
into the fat summer wool

The farmers went across the mountain
side by side
until
they saw each other no more

The previous night they had been in a hut
They borrowed it from distant sheep farmers
who they almost didn't know
they were family and
family's families

They spent the night there
The mattresses were mouldy with age and
terrific
cold nature

They met for supper
They were sheep farmers
They were friends
and friends of friends

They lit a fire in the cold
rusted stove
undressed layer after layer
in the damp, grey
smoke
until they sat in only their shirts

Their unnatural black hair
pasted to their foreheads
They loved each other laughing
They looked at each other
through thick spectacles

I remember

I remember
cracks, hollows and openings
Soft areas
around even softer
ground
I think of the scallop
the way it shows off
Red meat
under a pale surface
It dreams of
dancing
from its place
on the ocean floor
motionless
Far out
everything slants
towards the dark, the grey
I was there myself
just now
fourteen days ago
under your hands

I came down from the mountains

I came down from the mountains, without skis, without
clothes. I walked along a river and the damp felt cold against
the skin. I came down from the mountains. I had gone up
without supplies. I came down from the mountains like Jesus,
only weaker, more dead. I came down from the mountains,
but none the wiser. I had no parables to calm the storm
with. The stories felt light. The stories were like snow in my
hands, melted and poured with my cold sweat. It was no
warmer here, in the deep woods, between pines thicker than
men. I came down from the mountains and was let loose
in the woods, the mountains let me go. I came down from
the mountains like water. I thought the woods resembled
courtyards in cities. It smelt of rubbish, excrement and rotted
wood. I came down from the mountains. I slipped into the
courtyards like worms. I walked on, out through the gates that
were like openings in the wood. I left the big trees behind.
Between the big trees there was dense thicket. I came down
from the mountains. I was on level ground, in the streets. The
stories should set the day free. And so the poem came to

from *Outside the Institution*

THE OLD POET

The old poet lost his words
on the way up from the boathouse
to the dark forest edge where
stones lay in a pattern
he once understood

Some time afterwards the children
from neighbouring books came rushing in
And his pale
face turned away
from itself

The children thought they sat for a long time
while the old man
held his breath, groping for
heather to write with, something
savoury he could think about
until they left

He did not call after people
he knew or once had
seen on the road, but
whispered the names of those he wished
would proof read the patches of field
he called white sheets

He believed pain and farming
were the same thing, a word was not
a word. In the hospital
he dictated a hymn
to the white wall
behind the blue grapes

He did not believe books could
speak or love anyone
but he thought about the mouths
that could form words

My father has gone

My father has gone to the other side of the valley
He calls from the old phone booth by the village
road
The red metal booth which no one uses any more
The phone in the booth still works
Blind, my father searches for change in his pockets
He drops coins down through the bars in the floor
My father searches for coins with
his thin fingers with nails that are too long
He no longer has a working man's hands
He is re-educated, is between assignments
He has changed his life
He calls me, finally, I run to the phone
I know it is him
for I can tell by the shrill sound
which signifies lack of patience
When father calls I must come at once
He speaks to me without words
I hear his breath from far away
The line makes a crackling sound as if we were at war
My father does not know what to ask me
Despite this he asks me, casually
like a by-product of the crackling conversation
like a breath inside his own breath
am I still his son
Or am I another man?
Am I someone he does not know?
What do I want of him? he asks
He now has a new life
My father calls me up
but he cannot speak
I don't know why this surprises me
In fact, he has turned everything upside down

He roams the woods, he is still here
He jumps in a parachute, but never touches ground
He floats between heaven and earth
with a torn receiver in his hand

FATHER ASKS

Father asks who I am because he has become another
Father asks if I can come to him
because he does not know me
Father does not ask
he is old young
He is a wrinkled child, newly born
long ago

IVORY

You sit playing the piano
clinging to the planet
Your finger tips touching ivory
Somebody from another solar system
would never understand it
You get up
walk toward the black hole
by the front door

NIGHT

A light year travels past at speed
a shooting star on a quiet night
A party you never attended
Fire works you never saw
because you had other obligations
that New Year's Eve
You builder
thinker, firefly
in earth

TOURIST

When I looked out of the window I caught a glimpse of my
father, still young, standing in the garden cutting roses, something
he was good at
Dressed in green he wore a green cap with a black shade
I am certain it was him, his skin smooth, his hair slightly greying
his body light, strong, springy
He looked at each twig, each bud, closely considering
before he cut. I ran out, but when I reached the garden
he was gone, his place by the rose hedge empty
I ran to the basement where he often used to
change his clothes
or drink a beer
But when I reached the door I met a dark, strange woman
She was a German tourist, as it
happened, who said she had come to help
a sick child

A DOG WITH THREE EYES

I saw a dog with three eyes. He came with his master. Half
way over the third eye, on the side of the head, there was red
film. He tried pulling the film over his eye so as to blind it,
but couldn't manage it. The dog didn't feel that he needed
this eye. The eye was slant and pulled into a point at one end.
I could tell he was observing me with it. The dog walked
in circles and it looked as if he had trouble walking straight.
When I got further away from him I could see his head was
crooked, with one ear missing or very reduced. The dog was
helpless, governed by his third eye.

PHOTOS FROM THE WAR

In his room my father has photos from the war
nothing else, no grandchild, no woman
from happier days
In his room my father has photos from the war
a long time ago, but
he was already a grown man
In his room my father has photos from the war
no snapshots from his childhood
no father no mother nor a family
He rests in the war held firmly
by other soldiers
their smiles and joy
In his room my father has photos from the war
in the background
a parked bomber
and some way in front the soldiers
huddle around him

UPBRINGING

The crazy ones helped me
They came in the morning
I lay listening as they swarmed into the house
A whistling from the pipes when they turned on the taps
A roar from the stove when they lit the fire
As I got to my feet they made me breakfast
The heat from the stove struck my naked calves
They chopped eggs and let the coffee blend
They turned their eyes inside out
but did not miss the glass of milk
They each did their little part
They each had a small contribution
teaspoons, candles, napkins
They collaborated on weaving my clothes
Quick as lightning they sowed the day together
They knew very well where I was
They knew the house I lived in, and
the road leading to it
They came to take care of me
They had seen me grow and now
I was quite big
What they spoke were not words
Their words were meat
Their words were palate and tongue
the soft muscle
Their words were heart and uvula
spit they fizzled in the wind
They did not clear the breakfast table
Had no time for that
They finished what they did for me, I
was the day's good deed
I was their bad excuse
for fleeing

I was their troubled time
They threw me away, swept me away
and forgot about me
I was lost in their high speed
difficult measures, seven over eights, five over fours
syncopations, chords, a swing
in bodies, studied stereotypes, no
spent, decrepit
are better words
They ran into the woods, gaunt
while they bellowed
about everyone chasing them
They branded everyone as criminals
against mankind, evil
following in hot pursuit
They fled from my equals
They ran away from those I loved, with no sense
of nuance
They split my family
Only I found favour in
their high pulse, their
blood rich in oxygen
They looked at me briefly
to ensure
I had heat, water
before they sped on
They did not manage caring, no
they were not philanthropists, they
contributed something else
They came with a gift. Something elusive
but also eternal
In the evening the crazy ones returned
I was outside the house

They filed into view, a shattered
flock. They had
been out of sight, but never
out of mind
In the woods they had hunted themselves
At dusk they returned, driven
by shadows, plunging
into the dark, they never
complained, they did not know how
They had calmed down
their madness burnt out, transformed
to feathery grief
Suddenly they pressed up against me
They did not ask
how my day had been
They did not look at me
They knew my moves
the way they observed everything, mercilessly
like the surface of wounds, fear in the blood
without ever fixing their eyes on anything
They caught hold of me after fun and games
The evening chores were at hand, so
their plans were
connected
I had talked rubbish with my mates
I had been eagerly observing the girls'
patterns of motion
The crazy ones were
purposeless, useless, helpless
Their hands marked by working extensively
with nothing
a hard grasp
around nothing

Still they guided me
in the most important questions
They danced before me
away from me, soon
I was the one who followed them
They lured me into a little room
They groped for me with a thousand fingers
while they uttered friendly sounds
They pushed up against me
then leapt away. That is
all they could manage

HOMECOMING

The crazy ones are meek now they are not so crazy anymore
The crazy ones have calmed down because the black has been
cut out of them. Evil has been burnt away
Conversation has helped perhaps
Cautiously the crazy ones return from therapy
Smiling they look around the place
This is what it was like, they think
recognizing nothing
Tongues of fire do not hang from the sky
They do not encounter things that don't exist
along the roads. At last they find their way
to their houses, hunting for
switches
All is as they left it
No one has changed anything, people say
it is just green
growth, rotted boards
Can the crazy ones take care of themselves now
clean the house, find food?
What is where madness once was?
An unfurnished room?
White squares after pictures?
Silently the crazy ones sit in their chairs
scrutinizing me when I arrive

FINERY

Sentences block the poet's way
He sits with small words in his hands
glass pearls he was given as a child

Thought pouts after all these years
like a beautiful woman dressing up
for the sake of company

Explanations hide other explanations
old men pile on top of each other
in hotel receptions

Words flash over words
Why do I not write
about what I do not write about

A TURN FOR THE WORSE

The crazy ones have been out into the woods
now they are definitely
inside their houses
The crazy ones are crazier again
A whisper goes round in the village
How could it happen?
How could they build our shame
so sky high?
They were as I said in the woods
filling out dales, ravines, the space
between trees with
muffled cries
embracing themselves
when they thought
no one observed, if they
could think like that
with their crazy
minds, afflicted by
their speed, how they ran
bellowing songs, joyless arias
a wide register from coloratura to deep
bass. But then they left
the woods. Were they
tired? Had they
walked far?
Did they recognize
their own muscles?
Did they feel
their soles and the road
beneath their
blisters
was that
why they made

such faces
as they rushed toward
internal space. Leaving
behind a quiet village.
What was the village without madness?
What was the home without fear
of the self, deep down to
the bottom of the eyes
I could not love
my post-mad
village when the crazy ones
once more approached
their houses, but differently now, pur-
posefully, no
longer confused, taking on
a steady stride, this
day that passed into evening. The cows
bellowed by the gate, missing their
owner, clamouring
for a milkmaid
while
the crazy ones slipped
inside their doors
entrenching themselves

WORDS

Now the crazy ones have left their homes again
They couldn't stand being inside any longer
They come through the village in the twilight hour
tiptoeing like thieves
They don't want to make more noise
They try with all their might to be well again
They laugh and talk of nothing
For them that is like lifting a mountain
Under their arms they carry books
Now they are coming to me
They know I have gone to bed at this hour
They open their books and their mouths
They read to me
They form words inspired by the pages
or something they have in mind
They read about their own dark gaze
They tell me about what they are thinking now
things that spin
things that shine
things falling out of the sun's core
Night is near
Don't read any more
I say

THE ORDINARY

Now still some time
has passed
The crazy ones are not here
anymore. Their houses are deserted
left behind like snakes' skins
in a sunny place, or empty shells
on sandy beaches. I walk
in their gardens, overgrown, but
you can catch a glimpse of
cabbage gone to seed, remnants
of carrots, asparagus
has survived. Wave motions under
the tall grass
give witness of madness
or a strawberry field. Time
is the best psychiatrist
the years bring comfort to frightened mouths
quiets unconscious hands
Now I visit the crazy ones
in new places. Far out, further
in, away from the water
A glade in the woods can
be a parking lot. I don't
take those close to me along
but let them wait in the car
These are my obligations, my
dreams that slide through
the corridor. It is Sunday
soon the ferry will leave
for the other side. The crazy ones have
their own quarters, a grand hall
appears
a living room where they sit

pupated. They occupy wheel chairs, but
go nowhere, those times
are past. The crazy ones look
at me, we know you, they say
we know so well who you are
and you are welcome
here with us, they
continue
using their last words, the last sounds
they have. Are the crazy ones
crazy now? Have they
lost the heavy
brain muscle none could
exchange for grief?
Have they shrunk to
all that is ordinary close to
the bone, or does winter cabbage
still sprout in the heart?
I do not recognize
the crazy ones

THE CAR RIDE

1

The car charged the roof and walls in the old house with energy. It sprayed an innocent foam into the empty spaces so I could settle down. But the peace the car gave me was only temporary. I could stand stillness for a while because the car promised motion. Small bubbles emerged from the wires long after I had parked. The steel creaked and groaned while the engine bay cooled. Around the cylinder head gasket it perspired a bit of oil. It stood on the gravel, dead and pointless, without me. It laid its palms against the hard, sharp grains. Everything and everyone kept moving, except the car. It was a journey. The roads existed for it. At night the engine roared as quiet as ants under the flagstone.

2

I gave the car its dead life. I bought it for money I could have
spent more wisely, I drove it here, parked, placed it beside
those I love. I was an extension of factory streets, engineers,
robots' arms. I lay steel and details in plastic against soft skin.
I gave the car its quiet time by leaving it in the parking lot.
When I got back into the driver's seat the car was whole
again. I felt the combustion engine against the front of my
body. Those closest to me were with me. O time that steers
our movements towards heaven's gate. A wonderful series
of breaths which decide the time to start. We sat still for a
moment, waiting, while the car belched forth the future.

3

When the time comes the car takes off. Who can stop a steel
flower from spreading its storm-grey petals? Who can choke
the cold life by refusing it air and a permit? Who can stop the
wheel from singing the shiny song raw power composes. The
car overthrows the earth, turns up the fields like a plough the
size of a rat. Digging its snout into the strata of stone noticing
the heat that runs in the shafts. Who can throw themselves
out of a tin can as they chase rainbows and road signs? Who
can extinguish the fuel when it has caught fire in the heart of
the construction? And do not forget that motion is impossible,
driving is a wild, sad dream. Just ask Neil Armstrong, he
remained in the same spot, in the fine moon dust. Where shall
we live? the car asks.

4

In spring I changed wheels. I kicked loose the nuts that
had got stuck during the winter. The car on its knees in the
gravel as I fetched the summer tyres. Snow that fell last year
hung heavy in the air when we sped over the dry asphalt. We
drove past small round hollows of thought. The car brushed
the mountain sides like a kitten snuggling up to its mother.
The landscapes we went through leapt back like old people
on their way to fetch the post. The car had cleaned out the
woods, left behind a wide lane of sugar. I no longer heard
the roar of the motor mumbling. The ring of valve springs
danced through the air far behind me. I turned and turned
the steering wheel until I reached the grey light that envelops
the eyes.

5

I was standing on my two feet, without a car. In front of me lay a bright beach with a field. I walked through the grass, unsteady as a small child. Behind a tall fence, overgrown with green, was a big party. My best friends were getting married. I had no idea. I had never seen the place before. I forced my way among guests like a lost train conductor. They did not step aside. I crept inside, but they did not notice. I hurried past the crowd and down to the beach. The evening light had transformed the colours. Remnants of a warm day licked between my toes.

6

I closed my eyes and passed the crowd in the opposite
direction, without saying goodbye. I went through the gate
and heard the music die out, dwindle to a beat box. Some
way further on I stopped by a boulder, rested my hand on the
stone that reached my shoulder. The bride came after me, said
I must not leave. We need each other, to state the obvious, she
said. The boulder reached her hairline. She could not see the
top of it which seemed polished, but soiled by pigeon shit.
She said the groom had been through a difficult time lately.
That's why he is dressed in soft fabric, such as velvet. And only
strong colours, she added. I got into the car. The groom was
standing under a lamp post. The colours were wiped out near
the ground where the light was blurred. The bride stood by
the boulder. The party reached its climax.

7

I turned the ignition and childhood was over. I let go, was
thrown back against the neck pad, forward once more, and
swallowed my youth that poured out from the heater. I
left behind a hole in the yard. Deep down the deadlocked
crankshaft came loose. Roots of docks danced on the gravel. I
drove into intoxication and friendships, encapsulated by used
cars, stylised rust boxes, to the howl of wheel bearings, fan
belts, cassette players playing the same songs over and over.
I drove into communion, diluted as drivel, swerved through
curves, scraping crags that jutted out too far, crashing dance
floor after dance floor, deaf from electric music, empty bottles
rolling around the car.

8

I drove on the next day, in the morning, fetched by those
I had met the previous evening and must have made an
agreement with. I took over the wheel and drove to a girl,
long before she was up, passed her house, her swing, garage,
while the car almost died from speed humps and burnt oil.
She could have been in her bed, in the pyjama darkness,
behind closed lids, swollen from kisses she had no faith in.
She could have forgotten what she said to me, or did I speak
to her? She could have remembered it so well. I waited a
long time outside, the engine running, and my new friends
sleeping in the back seat, young, ruined. She did not come. So
I stepped on it and ran into a wall of reflection.

9

After a party we drove into the mountains. The mountains
stopped all music and cut off all hope. The mountains towered
and stilled thought. The roar of the engine crept between
stones. Water trickled through petrified grass. Silver grey
broccoli lined the slopes. The mountains kept silent till we
ran off the road, the oil sump hit the rock. Further ahead
we entered the road again, after manoeuvres we could not
account for. We drove to villages, hutted camps, space stations
archeologists knew nothing about. We drove to cooks,
household economists, cleaning assistants. As we woke them
up, they said we were expected. They served fried eggs and
coffee in the ice cold summer's night. All of us boys were a
combination of children and quiet men.

10

The car stood behind the barn. It was in summer and after
night, before morning. A time of day we had never seen
before. The car stood exactly where the dirt ran out below the
dung channel after spring farming that had not been done.
The thick running mass made all plants, rhubarb, goutweed,
hop, unnaturally green and lush. We sat crammed into the
car, completely still, breathing cold fjords on the inside of the
windows.

11

The others wanted me to drive. They came to fetch me in their own cars, purchased with what they had earned drilling rock or working metal by molten pools. They said they had no interest in cars, or picking up girls, but something simpler and greater. They sat drinking and talking about things they did not think I would understand. They told me where they wanted to go and I drove them out of the parish and along the fjord. I took them to dances and fights that burnt out before we drove on. I took them to valleys with lanes that were much too wide. We arrived at small farms without a name. I sat waiting for them while they visited girls living with their parents. Widows lay wide awake in adjacent rooms. The cattle asleep in outhouses.

12

I drove back in the opposite direction, over the mountain lakes, without passengers this time. I had no wheels, but insect feet. I did not cruise the dark quiet surface, but let it keep its deep secrets. I drove on, up on shore again, over the summer heath, without even touching the dew or the nectar of the bilberry flower. I could see myself on the horizon, crow black in the rear light or transparent, maybe all gone. Could I see anything at all as I rushed forward? Could I enjoy the sight of pebbles, cats killed on the road, twigs from last year? Could I study the fjord slurping the land on the other side?

13

Thank you and have a safe journey, somebody said. I got into the car, started and drove off. I drove right into the rain as if it was clear and the sun shone. I drove into garages and multi-storey car parks that did not exist. When I came to the last wall I stepped on the gas and drove on, into a quiet night. I drove along narrow roads in the dark, faster than the wet asphalt could come into being. I drove into mist or a mountain. I drove into a tunnel or a finely spun net of water drops. The mountain closed in. I encountered a silent, grey storm. I could no longer spot the rear lights of the car in front. A road man called out to me.

14

Fast or slow, it no longer mattered. I came clear of shadow, put the forest of my manhood behind me, where snow still lay among frail trees. I drove through early spring, a beautiful landscape, withered grass, dead remnants of plants, old firs dressed in sun. I was approaching the parish town, one hand casually on the wheel, the other on the arm rest. My car was new, though not quite, expensive, but not too expensive, well-equipped, but nothing unusual. I did not want to stand out. The shiny polish was covered in dust and dried up drifts from spring thaw, melt water.

15

I passed stylish petrol stations. I cruised through streets upgraded with Chinese granite curbstones and speed humps. I parked the car in a marked space and paid my ticket. The old church, freshly tarred, hovered above ruins. The power station was transformed into a picture gallery. From an ancient kitchen came the sound of soup, the only thing I recognized. Prams parked under trees. The sun baked the asphalt into soft oil. I went to the shop with the hard floor of cracked marble. You stood between the peppers and the honey dew melons, lost in the bright song of thought. You lived nowhere. I was home.

INVISIBLE

I went round town with the crazy ones
I often went with them on walks
or they kept me company
They gathered around me
They walked beside me
absentmindedly, controlled
by old habits
or indicators they were born with
The town was washed clean, white
by so much rain
Between us and the town's glass
was more glass
Under the dome of the sky
was another dome
more invisible than air
The crazy ones
were well behaved
They sang quietly
and studied
the leaves on the pavement
the cakes of sea urchins
the worms in the grass
They sat down with me in the park
I who had been their persecutor
evil spirit
I who had crammed them
into rooms
that were much too small
I had beaten them, pestered them
demanded they should know
incomprehensible rows of
letters, passwords
for serving places and

sleeping machines. Now
we look quite normal
I told them

I RETURN TO THE LANDSCAPE

I return to the landscape where the crazy ones once were
So much is altered, I can no longer see
the exercise yards where they wandered restless
or sat curled up by the concrete wall
Even the houses they lived in have been torn down
or reconstructed and the absence of madness strikes me
I remember when I first met the crazy ones
their wild gaze, high pitched howls and they ran
right up to me and far away
What did they see with their eyes open wide
What can they have noticed from the corner of their eyes
What did the crazy ones see without seeing
What traces of them in the inconceivable
landscape in the landscape

Loss

I've heard that my father has also
come back. Someone has spotted
him on the boat. He stood on deck
in uniform. He smoked an English cigarette
and called all the mountains
by name. He had missed them so much.
I think it was him I saw yesterday
when he walked between the trees
in the peaceful darkness
he had waited for
a freehold privilege
a beautiful smallholding
I never knew about

QUESTION

In your eye, child, I saw the question you could not
articulate, the question you fled from
with movements cut out of happy days you had never seen
only inherited from the vast darkness beneath us
Your joy that seemed like weeping, jumps and leaps
resembling a landslide of light and voices, small as you were
You ran in and out of rooms with
energy that never declined

I saw in your eyes, child, pain that you did not know
anything about, howls you pushed inches away
sheer drops where you balanced, vacantly. How
could I imagine a way into your
submarine forests of grass
or meet you
in cold, uninitiated cathedrals

To the institution

I took you to the institution
You held my hand, the only
reliable thing. Did I sense an encouraging squeeze
from your fingers? Or were your palms
calmer than I had ever known them? I interpreted
your movements, your hair, yes
the clothes I myself had chosen, dressed you in
I interpreted each breath, each step. Blindly
I walked with you across the
open square in front of a yellow wall
I saw no patterns in the gravel, no
birds descended, no signs brushed
against me, no faith supported me
only the one thought
of you, the playful child
imprisoned inside you. Let me
explain. The thought of you
preceded me. The thought was
already inside the institution. The door
opened. We were
in the hall. I had already
started using the institutional language
before it had closed its walls around us
The explanations were already lodged
inside me. I saw the plans
notices, diagrams, ob-
jectives. They should
help you. I heard the
clear, ugly song. I saw your tears
in the wrong places, inexplicably
flowing, not to be reached
with hands. I wanted to thank

you. There's really nothing
to thank me for
you said

PARTING

I lost my language at the institution
You were gone when I left you there
you entered the surprisingly dark recreation rooms
I lost my language in the hour of parting
which I so much feared. All words
rolled together with you, speechless child
It was as if you could play
with a ball or words or the shadows of
the other speechless children
who fled
The institution gave me new words

ON THE WAY TO THE CAR

How can I describe the institution with words
that are not approved by the institution
How can I describe the row of windows I
turn away from walking towards the car
I should have seen
you there behind the glass, the wall, what
you were closed in by
Your loneliness should have said goodbye
How can I describe you
with words the institution gave me, sucked
into me by hope

THE CONFERENCE ROOM

Why did I not see the institution with your eyes
Why did I not see you with my own eyes
Can I blame the institution
When I returned I did not visit you
did not interfere with your seconds
did not interrupt your vision
I walked across the empty sphere
outside the room you were in, ran
along the blue timber wall
and came to the conference room
charts for happiness
columns for sleep
I kept silent for I must not
let truth come out

THE BLIND SPOT

Who has placed the institution
among the other houses
The path leads past the blind spot
The stairs leading up say nothing
of those who live here, their mistakes
or promises in their blood
Worn shoes are still placed
on a wooden shelf, kitchen cupboards are
yellow pine, exactly as
it should be, mackerel fillet
on the table, tinned paté
further in are bedrooms, accurately furnished
as bedrooms, teddy bears set out
according to an agreed plan
Colourful curtains celebrate
a home. In the staff wardrobe boots
raincoats, quite ordinary jackets, further
away are cars, pedestrians, people
who are together
hurts me

MOVEMENTS

Twenty five years have passed
You were gone
most of the time
You were taken from me
I took you away from myself
How is your life at the institution?
I did not imagine how you were
Thought stopped at the institution
Thought circled around you
Thought could not enter your eyes
I did not manage to be with you
All I could see were movements
an artificial space around you
The institution cheered
it praised me

LUNCH

I accepted
the offer of lunch and talked with ease
across the table about all the ordinary things that
for you were not so ordinary. I felt the loss
of your contribution to the meal even though
you had set out
plates only aided by a picture plan
and clear instructions. There was something
I did not speak about. There were words waiting
for me. It was perhaps
the same words that waited for you
The same sounds were taken from us
My heart was
more closed than yours. Write
with your heart somebody
told me
That is what you did

9 7 8 1 8 4 8 6 1 0 7 5 0